Afterwards

The National Poetry Series 1984

Amy Bartlett
Afterwards
Selected by Galway Kinnell

Kathy Fagan
The Raft
Selected by Daniel Halpern

Robert L. Jones
Wild Onion
Selected by Carolyn Forché

Nathaniel Mackey
Eroding Witness
Selected by Michael Harper

Bruce Smith
Silver and Information
Selected by Hayden Carruth

Amy Bartlett

Afterwards

Persea Books
New York

For information, contact the publisher:
Persea Books
225 Lafayette Street
New York, N.Y. 10012

Acknowledgments: "Tryst" and "Gypsy Moths"
appeared in *Mudfish 1984.*
"Afterwards," "My Sister," "The Walk," and
"A Window on the Ground" appeared in
Ironwood 25 (Vol. 13, No. 1).

Designed by Peter St. John Ginna
Set in Sabon by Keystrokes, Lenox, Mass.

Library of Congress Cataloging in Publication Data

Bartlett, Amy.
Afterwards.

(The National poetry series)
I. Title. II. Series.
PS3552.A765A68   1985   811'.54   84-27267
ISBN 0-89255-090-2
ISBN 0-89255-091-0 (pbk.)

The National Poetry Series was established in 1978 to publish
five collections of poetry annually through five participating
publishers. The manuscripts are selected by five poets of national
reputation. Publication is funded by James A. Michener, Edward J.
Piszek, The Ford Foundation, The Witter Bynner Foundation, and
the five publishers—E.P. Dutton, Graywolf Press, Persea Books,
University of Georgia Press, and University of Illinois Press.

Contents

For my mother and my father

From My Window

Columns of light slant away
from the bridge in the water
as if there were a room down there
and heaven were not above, but below.
From backyards come the voices of children
and as if my own mother were chanting
me back to childhood, the faint voice
of a woman crying a name again and again.
Church bells—four, five, six times—
fade up there among the pigeons. Those
I have loved left blurred footprints
in the snow, going off in directions
I could not understand. I try to think
of them here—breaths off the river.

How the lamps in the dusk
shine with a richer yellow part way out
onto the terrace below—but just beyond
the dark, the trees and all the faces
are waiting. Now, up here in this air
too pure yet to hold the darkness,
I want to live like the woodsman

led by lamps that lighted and dimmed themselves
as he passed, or like the child who dreams
she cannot step out from between
the tracks but does and lets the spell
of wandering overtake her, inventing a way
through the woods—until the moment when my mother
and father return as the one person
they will become in death. They bring
the elderbark cradle where I will curl
into the shape in which my mother has lain.
And I will rock all the way back
to childhood, the moments of my life
clear as though on the other side of glass, as they pass,
giving back to existence a substance
that leaves me like steam. Then those
I have loved who have died before me
will step forward, and standing
around the crib, godmothers and godfathers,
say to one another—"That's not she,
no she is somewhere else."

Now

Sometimes we still make love—
his body haloed by my breath
turns the night damp and glittery,
as if lit by the radium stars
fixed to his boyhood ceiling
by a mother who would die of cancer,
the moon and Saturn ticking off
her time in half-lives,
raveling something
young and intricate in him.
He wraps each misfortune
around himself, and holds it against me,
while thoughts of his past
turn on their own above our bed.
Orphaned at twelve,
parceled out to military schools,
where women have faces of parchment,
the complexity of his need has sewn
me to him—dark threads running out and back—
so that when he twists,
I bend to keep from tearing.

Snow

Sometimes the winter sun
makes me think I remember
and turn to look for him—
a shape of light beside me;
or a sudden warmth—
something my body recalls.
But time falls—snow
descends into strange
humped shapes that make us say
that's the woodpile, that's the tree,
and whole days, weeks of our life together,
afternoons spent making love
become unrecognizable,
so that I say, "This is what happened,
this is how we felt,"
without coming close to what it was.

On the Observation Deck of the Empire State Building

This is the autumnal equinox,
but already night is rising, darkening
the thick smog like an ingredient
stirred from below. From the edge
I peer down at the city lights
the way sometimes I can see
all the way back to my childhood
down those streets at the end of the day
curiously quiet, except for a ball
bouncing again and again.
And I feel as when a child of three or four
I balanced at the top of the cellar stairs
until I felt a tug I didn't understand
and then pulled myself back.
And now I feel the feeling
I knew on spring afternoons
when I stood at my upstairs window
and let the air blow over me
and felt set apart from my self by life itself
and by another knowledge

acrid, like the smell of the metal screen
against my face. Later, I climbed fire towers
and tops of tall buildings, clinging
to the handrails, watching
the ground leave me through gaps
between the steps, until
the land fell away into hills I had never seen
like a cloth shaken out and smoothed.

On the Eiffel Tower last summer
when failures in love felt like finding
again and again the one rotting step,
I climbed up and down, seeking
that shaky vertigo, the odd perspectives
a turn of events can give—
the sight of my life whole and yet oblique
like the buildings of Les Invalides;
seeking a sense of separateness,
of animal finiteness and fear:
one set of days lived,
the other whole and unformed
before me, like a point of equilibrium
where I could balance.
And I almost willed it to happen
as if I could plunge right then,
like the crazy boy, holding my treasure—
everything I had left.

—

Back inside the people give off warmth
by their numerous presence
and I let myself be comforted by their voices
unfocused and indistinct
the way I never could if I were listening.
Through the glass, the sky seems even more pale
and full of light, like the ceiling
of a room still lit after the guests have left.

Walking Home

As I walk here among the young
swamp maples, my shadow
follows me, an intense piece of darkness.
The river glitters idly through the trees
as if with its own source of light.
Visible now from miles away,
it is always there on the edge of sight
like something true not always acknowledged.
So much more light
shines through the trees,
that I can almost see the dead
sitting cross-legged
under the earth. Their words
have been taken away from them.
They crouch over themselves
as if to warm their limbs
but their touch is cold.
Blowing on their hands,
they move into a circle
as if around a storyteller and a fire.

Up through the falling leaves
in the empty branches
one can see nests still held fast,
squirrels' nests thick
with last winter's leaves
and robins' nests, compact and fine
as if woven out of human hair.
Last summer sleeping in an upper room
I woke to hear voices mingling
faraway and indistinct.
Watching shadows move across
the trapezoids of light
that widened away from the house
I felt for a moment as I did
when as a child I lay awake
and looked up out of my window at the branches
darker than the sky,
and felt safe from any harm
because my parents' voices were murmuring.

My nephews are grown and changed—
the older one, tall, narrow, blond
goes to school this year;
the younger one has hair
the color of the hemlock needles
on the floor of the woods

that with age will darken
to the color of fallen acorns.
When I look into their eyes,
I know that I, not they,
will walk ahead down a road
that goes into a woods
where the tops of the trees
shut out the sky and the wind
soundlessly lifts the branches.

Now the grasses are covered
with a fine white vapor
that transcends them individually
like that ghostly white
of the heads of very old people
when they all sit near each other at church.
In the woods darkness
is waiting among the hemlocks—
their lower branches dry and brittle—
darkness that is without a seam
like that which brings together ocean and sky.
When I was a child, the windows
became all black from the inside,
and then the steam of cooking
fogged them evenly and white

and everything—trees, bushes—fell away
from the house until only
the house and the night were left.

One Childhood

A field of dark brown leaves
extends down into the swamp
where the snow is old, shrunken
and covered with a fine, black dust.
Under the firs, the needles
are dry and soft as a child's hair;
the oak leaves are brittle,
glossy and veined—small dried skeletons
we would toss into the air.

The house is so close to the river
the water shines in at the windows.
And now, as if it were a second day,
the moon is polishing the river, like foil,
but like a failed mother
does not bring out color of any kind.
And the house is opened by light;
it crosses the floor, enters
the rooms, lights them again:
the turn in the stairs
is resolving an emotion.
The glance that takes in the oak bent

over the river brings a thought
to its conclusion. Reaching-the-landing
means the feeling subsides.
Entering one room is crossing
over into another emotion—sometimes
it is filled with light;
sometimes it is a waiting silence.

Now the house goes out
room by room, one for each of the lives
that will have been—until a single light
burns in an upper window—
a life lived intensely and alone.

Camping Out

A moon rises with Venus, its companion star,
diffusely lighting the sky.
The water and stones shine.
The trees shine dark and silver,
and in the woods wait the silent camps
of darkness. Only the motion of water
rises heavily against the rocks,
like a pregnant woman undulating,
responding reluctantly to something within.
The empty summer houses
are like campfires gone out
on their bare sites along the shore.
Here how I have lived, or not lived
seems not to be important.
All of this will go on
no matter what I learn too late.

At Dusk

The immaculate house
presents an ordered, tended picture
secure in what it is,
like happiness achieved,
as if time were caught,
a precious liquid in a cup,
and held to the light
in a room where at dusk
the lamps burn low and evenly
and the family gathers, to be glimpsed
perhaps by someone passing
as people are seen at an accident
standing to the side and bending over
curious, intent, motionless, unable to assist.

Across the River

The tops of trees
are obscured by mist
and by broad lower branches.
The soft ground clasps my shoe
like a hand from below. Trunks appear
ahead then vanish several feet behind.
For a moment they all seem imagined,
that juniper bush clotted with snow,
these shoots of ground pine,
that leaf poking through snow, the mist
folded over the hill
like the flap of an envelope.
Darkness enters the mist
like drops of ink dissolving
into water. There is the sound
of metal knocking against the stone.
The river, darker than the sky,
is an even, moving blackness.
The moon, arbitrarily sliced in half
puts a glittering track of light

across it. Ahead, a person
emerges from the woods like a piece
of darkness separating itself
from the night. The small identical lights
suspended along the road above the valley
seem to say every life down here is the same.

Rindge, New Hampshire

The false lily of the valley
blooms this time of year.
Everything is new and pushes
upward; the ferns face all one way.
I go for walks on the paths
here, as I used to near my home,
expecting, as then, to feel
their different stages
their beginnings, middles and ends.
Everything is rainy and wet.
A small stream goes down a hill
into a crevice. The sky is low.
I am more than thirty years old,
and now when I come to the woods
I remain what I am; things seem less.
The small dry leaves scraping
back and forth repeat a phrase
in a language I cannot understand.
I remember dark nights when snow
like startling bits of calcium
materialized out of nothing and shone
in the wedge of light from the opened door

then vanished as if the dark were eating it.
We would know it was there
by the soundlessness and then the rush of wind
that seemed to want to speak to us,
reminding me of my grandfather when,
from his white bed, he turned his face toward me
and repeated sounds over and over
as if saying them again would make me understand.
At dusk, the sky would come down
to the edge of the river as if to drink,
the snow would disappear before it hit the water.
The river was gray at the edges
but in the middle, glossy, black,
as if reflecting the bottom, not the sky,
or as if a dark eye had opened
where summer weeds still moved over the stones.

Early August

Last night the mist coming over the hills
and down through the valley
let through the light of goldenrod,
just now new yellow-green,
of black-eyed susans, and of clover
like faint stars burning through—
and blew on, cold, to the hills beyond.
As we ate the sky hardened
into low clouds, the windows darkened
until there were twelve squares of dark
everywhere one looked,
as if all of space were out there suddenly,
and our forms rippled in the glass.

He took my hand, his hands warm and dry.
His hair fell around his face
and I was curious, his face for a moment
became emotional, feminine.
Then he pressed against me,
his soft flannel shirt was on my cheek.
I was neither reluctant nor avid.
We more undressed, his eyes

emptied of sight, intent not on me,
but on something beyond, like me.
Later, the clouds moved off;
their faint gray shapes decamped
across the dark sky. And in the kitchen,
scraping the plates, suddenly I saw the stars,
the way the mind grasps what is real
or some idea or truth only in moments
as if they had been waiting for us all along.

3:00 A.M.

Five bodies are lying
as if on altars, or on clouds,
yielding themselves up to sleep
more certainly than ever
to each other or to me.
They seem so approachable—
as when a child I was made
reverent by a hush at the table,
by a silence among adults,
as if I could touch
for that one moment, the shape
of their being, mysterious
and separate from me
like the rim of the table I held.

Mudfish

Like fish we played
head to tail, under blankets
stretched across chairs,
while our parents lumbered
like gods through the rooms
above us. And we made magic
with pine needles and boughs
in secret circles in the woods,
whispering stories.
Then we were close to each other
and to the sun,
and the trees could hear.
At night we tried to feel
our parents' moods—huge mouths
open in laughter or anger,
the dark roofs like the nave of our church,
large gold teeth in the back.

On Sundays

On Sundays, my father tied
my brother John's tie. As he looped
the tie over itself, gently
sliding the knot upwards,
the moment settled around him
and spread out touching us all,
so that we stood hushed, open-mouthed,
hungrily watching him thread
the tie back and through,
as if we could catch
and dissolve on our tongues
this wafer of our father's care,
a moment of swift, delicate fingers.

Bridgewater State Hospital

Here, concertina wire circles
endlessly along a chain link fence
like the rationalizations of a thief.
Shuddering with electric current
the heavy metal doors swing open.
An airport scanner searches me to the bone.
Bent over like a shy crane, he smiles,
but looks away. As we talk,
he seems to watch each phrase
disappearing into the air.
In his silences I think I hear doors
click shut on empty closets,
or see his thoughts—dull light
wavering across a pale ceiling.
Light, was it light or noise—
the boat's sulphur beams poking
down the long reluctant river,
or its motor startling the trees
naked and unaware—
that forced copulating animals
to part and run for dark?
When he pitched the cinder block

off the bridge his arms sprang out,
his body seemed to plummet
end over end toward the boat,
his mouth was peeled back
like fruit by their screams.

The Walk

Walking past the neighbor's house
I remember how it was then—shrunken
into snow as if for warmth.
I remember walking past the skating pond
frozen between hills, through the ghostly
white swamp, and, in coldest weather, across
the gray ice of the river. Here
is the burned-out house, where rain
wetted fireplace stones. Then it was
I felt I could walk beyond the darkness
and see and feel everywhere
like that moment when the station
and then lighted houses
slip from the departing passenger.
Sometimes he came with me, hunched
over himself, falling behind, so quiet
I would forget him, and then
it would be as if one of the trees
stirred itself and fell into step with me.
Now we come to the road's end
and there is no path to follow.
I think he is walking away, waist-deep

through tow-headed summer fields.
I remember he always strayed from me,
walking back out of memory.
But when I get home and open the door
he is there, leaning on the doorframe
of the darkened kitchen, come back to me,
hands part way through an action
they have forgotten,
the frayed jacket over an arm.

The Visiting Hour

He holds his face straight ahead,
but looks out of the corner of his eyes
like a horse, or like one who has come back
from the other side. Now he sits sideways
on the chair, curled over himself,
his head down, his neck almost parallel
to the ground as if protecting the source
of whatever mysteries arise from within.
When he looks up, his eyes seem to be trying
to roll back to let him gaze inward.
I remember once glimpsing him among the trees
at night, naked but for a towel at his waist,
a shape lighter than anything else,
his pale skin shining as never in the day,
silent, intent upon not disturbing
some presence in the dark. Today,
he is silent like the very old
who listen, but have no more to say in this world,
or like the people I once saw standing
motionless on a lawn high above me,
dappled by summer light, here and not here.
When it is time to go, I turn away

—

from him, as from a campfire
I have hovered over, unable to get it going.

Driving away, I keep seeing the house;
each room is alight with unseen lamps
showing on the walls, but no one is there—
one of the succession of the lights through time that,
like a row of street lamps, together
lay down on the past the way back
to those afternoons and the piano, when he played
with a discipline that transcended all others.
There he sits, his hands above the keys,
his head turned so I cannot see the face,
and I am waiting for him to play a passage
of that low, measured music which moves
through us at unexpected times
on our way alone toward death.
Those in the room pause; our hands
stop midway through what they are doing
and we turn our heads to the window
to look at nothing, and quieted
like hens stroked motionless, we let
the music pass over us like the wind.
I want to reach back and close the lights
that show me this, like candles on the dinner table
that shine in the even panes of blackness

after everybody has driven off down
the funnel of darkness between the trees—
and leave our childhood dark.

In our life here, sometimes a young man
with our dark blond hair and slight frame
walks past me, and I might briefly follow him
but not too closely, so the illusion won't be broken.
Or I'm startled by one of two forms
their bodies gone slack over a subway grate,
slumped there like two sacks of grain
leaning into each other. Or sometimes
at the corner, on a January night,
one I seem to know is lying against a wall,
finished with wandering, all his strength
given out under him right there.

Gypsy Moths

After dark, my father paints a band of tar
around each tree. "They're bad this year."
A grandchild and now his son-in-law are gone.
As he angles his broom toward the high eaten branches,
I wonder if he sees my sister, patient, stationary,
her life that fragile and intricate.

Elegy

I remember his perfection,
the perfection God gives, of God's eyes—
consciousness looking out at me—
how they seemed to know
what we ourselves see only in moments.
I remember his brow wrinkled
to the center; I remember my hands musing
on their own over his skin.
What he left us is rooms,
seen suddenly obliquely,
as if from above, each lighted
with one light. In them we stand
off to the side of each other
and there are long corridors
down which somewhere, someone
sits reading a small book alone.

For my nephew Bertram Connelly, June–August, 1978

The Funerals

I remember the slow passage
of the hearse and cars along
the roads and lanes of Old Town.
Sometimes we saw only the tops
riding above the roadside bushes
and the procession seemed to be moving
with a power not its own, like flowers
floating on water, until it slowed
and stopped at the cemetery. I remember
how every sound became significant,
like a scrap of paper dropped by a child
from a bridge and watched for
on the other side. I remember the hay bales
like coffins in the fields, and how at evening
the sun burned through the grasses
casting long shadows—all of those
experiences for which there are no words.

My Sister

I see her in a house
among fields going back to woods,
three years after the last word
has passed between us, on a day
like this one—sky full of unfallen snow,
the gray river reflecting nothing,
everywhere the brown and white
of small trees, the tiny blanks of snow.

I think I see her. She has strayed
too far for me to follow
out through fields like the angular
landscapes she last painted.
Each of us moves in small daily ways
in rooms that grow larger,
with more distances to walk
between the chairs, amid silences
that are listening for the least sound
one of us makes. Sometimes I feel her
watching me not without love, her dark house
a shell over her, the windows

so large they seem to touch the ground.
And I wish we could come together again
and light the kerosene lamps
and talk our lives backward
like us in childhood feeling our way
to bed in the dark.

A Window on the Ground

The light reaches us from a long way off.
Under the bridge, a thin veined skin of ice
is forming on the open water
like the beginning of healing.
My sister and I walk between the slopes of snow
past the dark, extinguished houses
each a lamp gone out—
and see the unrevealing windows
that reflect back the scene
but with a hint of darkness underneath
like a scrim—the way a change of light
will reveal an interior, a room behind.
When I speak she answers too briefly;
her face has sunk down to the bone and turned old.
We walk among the tops of trees
over the frozen flooded marsh, conscious
of another life beneath us
as we were in childhood—
of fish sometimes, of the golden apples,
the dogs with their big eyes.
She strays behind and a little
to the left of me over the gray ice,

putting the distance that is always there
between us. Her head
is down and turned slightly away
as if she were searching the ice
for tracks—the way when they make mystery
children follow each other's paper trails
through the wood. But there are only
the little pillows of snow
and the series of small waves frozen
in a single motion forward
like the beginning of sisterly affection.
And here, on the other side of this river
with its paths circling back on themselves
like one lost, is the site
of the burned-down house
with the chimney remaining
as if the house had consumed itself
piece by piece in the fireplace.
My sister angles her face, like a blind person,
sensing some silence. For weeks
after the funeral she played the funeral song
over and over, sitting still,
blind-looking at something beyond me.
I loved her then. I always faced her
and paid close attention to what I imagined she felt.
I remember how her son Louis, when he heard steps

would run to the window, crying, "Ot, Ot,"
happy again suddenly until he saw
it was not his father's face.
When we sorted out her husband's possessions
together, we could feel their impassivity,
how unable, though worn and hunched to his shape
they were to reveal their memories.
For a long time after I returned home,
when I would lie down at night,
I would suddenly sense all she was experiencing.
Now she has heard the music of heaven
from within and so only half listens,
the way I have in cathedrals.
She is one who loves truth so much
mostly only silence matters or can be true.
Her bones show, as if grief
had worked into the skeleton.

She bends down and brushes
away the soft layer of snow
where the ice is smooth, dark
filled with faint white air
bubbles like the sky in early evening.
She kneels, putting her hands on either side
of her face, I think she looks

through the window on the ground
she has found at last on the water,
at blurred shapes in the rooms of dark water.

My Father Napping

His head lolls forward like a rag doll's;
his arms are held tight against his sides
the way one day they will be forever—
until and after they are bones;
his legs are pressed together
and turned to the side, knees
and feet pointing the same way—
like a girl riding sidesaddle.
I remember on a hot spring afternoon
coming to a friend's barn
and pausing at the threshold;
the space seemed to contain
the whole afternoon within it.
The light stretched dimly up
to the rafters where I could not see,
and in the dark corners I sensed
something about the life around me
I did not want to know.
He stirs, his eyes flutter
open, then close. One day someone else
may look out a window
and feel as I do now—

that I and not my father
am moving out on the swelling dusk
where the fireflies are blinking
first here and then unpredictably
to the right or left.

On a Sixty-Fifth Birthday

Take me to the ship where you go
every time I ask a question,
the ship with high white sides
impossible to scale, the vision
of open water you see
a little to the right or left of me.
Take me past the cabins—rows
of emptinesses—past the state-rooms
with their empty-lapped chairs,
past the kitchen
with its dry, long-necked faucets
and stacks of faceless
saucers and plates. Take me with you
to the hold, where above
the rusted keel there is only
the waiting darkness
and the grinding of what is left
of old ships over the reef.

For my father

Spring

The air today is a presence
like smoke from small fires
rising and blurring through the trees.
The cold exhalation of the woods
comes over me in small gasps
against my face, like the last breaths
of one who is dying escaping back
into the room. From far away comes the sound
of a chain saw working its gritted note
up the scale, then letting it fall,
then forcing it up again. It begins
to rain. Small drops intermittently
hit my head with the taps of single fingers—
the touch of a child, or the unconscious
gentle touch of a preoccupied mother.
Drops spring from the river's skin
and from the house come the thrumps
hitting a hollow space regularly
like a sound always present.
From the ground comes the humid scent
of leaves partway decayed and now exhumed—
a particular odor surrounding

someone loved, that one can step into.
Up to now, my father's body
has been indistinct, important
for the aura of personality
surrounding it, like an icon or shrine.
But as I walk past the bedroom
on the ground floor, which he uses now,
and see him stretched out
on his grandson's narrow single bed
and my mother dressing the incision,
his body does not look very much different
from a lover's even though it is yellowed
and the skin is slack from lost flesh
and like a shirt that is too large
pulls all in one direction.
I can't help thinking of the leaves
which covered the animal graveyard
when we were children. I remember
the skeletons of birds felt through down,
like tiny cricket cages,
and the exquisite constructions of chipmunks
felt through fur. As she washes him,
he looks happier, just as the animals
used to fall under the spell of our touch,
giving themselves over to us completely.

Once when we found a bird and thought it healed,
we put him on the branch of a tree
and it was true, some hours later he was gone.

Cafe Divino

Hunched shyly over the table,
she looks out at me like the raccoon
we used to catch eating in the light
from the open door on the porch,
a small disk in each eye
reflecting it back. When I ask a question
she answers in a word or two
then goes back to eating
as that raccoon used to,
turning the morsel of food
over itself in its small paws,
nibbling at the edges, its jaw
working under the furred skin—
looking up at the light, poised to run.
When she goes to the ladies' room
I must let her, the way
she must have decided years ago
to let me go by myself,
mentally following me all the way
to the door and then back
measuring the time it should take.

Tenebrae

Tonight a grandmother is dying
alone. The small lights
are being snuffed out
one by one—the hooded
faces, old, yet memory smooth
coming kindly forward then bowing
and backing away. And each
small flame extinguished
leaves its own new darkness,
the presence of something lost
yet sensed to be there still,
like trees hovering overhead
after switching off car lights—
a room of known shapes
just gone dark.

For Christine Moore Price, 1899–1982

Afterwards

The hills stiffen briefly
into shadow, leaving small lights
in dusk like the river ice
outside my childhood house
in which lights plotted a distance
to a point that has always seemed
safely out of reach. We look out
from the train at small towns,
then close suburban houses
lighted as if with one light,
then graveyards in which stones
rotate to look, and quarries
with water so dark they seem
to hold all our past in them—
Mimi, when I helped you dress, I felt
a man's shyness and awkwardness;
when I helped you down to the landing
you paused facing the frozen garden,
the withered nasturtiums,
and I held in my arms a shape
slightly larger than you
as I tried to feel what I could feel.

But I grew afraid as in that moment
between two people before anything is said.
The train sheds its little squares of light
into the weeds. I have explained
myself to one or two others,
have spoken when the words came.

For Miriam Bartlett, 1922–1983

Tryst

There has been a mistake
and you didn't die.
This time we meet
and love, like trees
in winter clashing
in a white waste of snow.
Your dark fingers
whisper against my face.

Love with the Same Name

For my cousin Mark Bartlett, 1948–1970

Sometimes when I hear
the silence of streets
the emptiness of rooms,
I try to listen for the crash—
waiting intently to hear it
as no one could have been that night
twelve years ago when a white car
cried fast down El Camino Real.

Afterwards, I thought
that if the world
were so imperfect
as to let you die
then I would fight back
by being perfect,
the perfect friend,
daughter, student,
sister, niece—
but no, not the perfect lover,

for the heart and lungs
became glass;
turned into something
that must not respond, that needs
only its other half.

The summer after you died, I drove
the grid of streets in Palo Alto
where corners lead only to more corners
and parallel lines to parallel lines.
In my apartment, I touched my face,
seeking myself in mirrors, in windows
looking out on exactly what was there—
as if I had become the panes
through which I could see but not feel
each experience that passed.

And in the autumn, I walked at night
through falling leaves
under black branches
from lighted building to lighted building.
Inside, the bright rooms and faces
brought forth too much the watery
darkness on the other side of the glass,
and I stayed just long enough
to feel that human warmth

—

before any complication
of thought or emotion,
like touching just with the fingertips.
But I felt whole only
when I could know night
completely descended over the earth
and the sky a dark
comprehending above me.

Once, camping beside a barn I thought deserted
on my way across country, I woke
to find every window lighted
and the pigs screaming
with a foreknowledge of death.
I drove all the way back to New York
as if I could drive through my whole
future and through all of yours
and come to the impossible meeting
of parallel lines where I would lie down
with that animal certainty of death—
as once I did with you,
your hair catching the lamplight,
your eyes giving me back
my own complete self-knowledge,
my hands on your shoulders and face

———
64

until I felt perfectly supported
like a body held by contours of sand.

Love with the same name
my other half
twelve years in ashes
dispersed
to my father's brother's land—
love in flower
in leaf, tree, stem, branch
bush
in moss, taut,
with jutting red flowers—
I remember coming downstairs
to find you in the dark
where you wanted to be—
we would sit together
our words slowing
until our thought formed
all the shapes around us,
the silence,
and the sky became thin
as the shell of consciousness.
Then love took language
back to its origin,
and speaking

was a touching of hands,
and everything seemed
like us, lighted
from within by its own being.